VIDEO GAME CODING

by Janet Slingerland

FOCUS READERS

WWW.FOCUSREADERS.COM

Focus Readers is distributed by North Star Editions:
sales@northstareditions.com | 888-417-0195

Produced for Focus Readers by Red Line Editorial.

Content Consultant: Dr. Sherali Zeadally, Associate Professor, College of Communication and Information, University of Kentucky

Photographs ©: sezer66/Shutterstock Images, cover, 1; pagadesign/iStockphoto, 4–5; Jacek Chabraszewski/Shutterstock Images, 7; Ain Mikail/Shutterstock Images, 8–9; Vector1st/Shutterstock Images, 11; chuckchee/Shutterstock Images, 13; Dragon Images/Shutterstock Images, 14–15; Tero Vesalainen/Shutterstock Images, 16; Liu zishan/Shutterstock Images, 19; georgeclerk/iStockphoto, 20–21; Nearbirds/Shutterstock Images, 23; Gorodenkoff/Shutterstock Images, 25; rkl_foto/Shutterstock Images, 26–27; Red Line Editorial, 29

Library of Congress Cataloging-in-Publication Data
Library of Congress Cataloging-in-Publication Data is available on the Library of Congress website.

ISBN
978-1-64185-329-3 (hardcover)
978-1-64185-387-3 (paperback)
978-1-64185-503-7 (ebook pdf)
978-1-64185-445-0 (hosted ebook)

Printed in the United States of America
Mankato, MN
October, 2018

ABOUT THE AUTHOR

Before writing books, Janet Slingerland was an engineer. She wrote code that was embedded in things such as telephones, submarines, and airplanes. She lives in New Jersey with her husband, three children, and a dog.

TABLE OF CONTENTS

CHAPTER 1

A Video Game World 5

CHAPTER 2

Game Design 9

CHAPTER 3

Bringing the Game to Life 15

CODING IN ACTION

Rendering 18

CHAPTER 4

Types of Coders 21

CHAPTER 5

Finishing Touches 27

Focus on Video Game Coding • 30
Glossary • 31
To Learn More • 32
Index • 32

A VIDEO GAME WORLD

Go-carts race across the TV's screen. They swerve around obstacles and launch off jumps. Players hold controllers shaped like steering wheels. They press a button on the side to make the go-carts move faster. Suddenly, a tree falls across the track. Players press another button to slam on the brakes.

Video games respond to players and track their scores.

Sometimes coins appear on the track. Players can steer their go-carts into the coins to collect them. Some coins boost players' speed. Others give them weapons that slow down their opponents. Exciting music plays in the background as they race toward the finish line.

BEHIND THE SCENES

There are many kinds of video games. Some video games are played on **consoles**. Some games run on smartphones or computers. Other games are played on small, handheld devices. All these games run using code. Code tells each device how to display the game's sounds and images. It also allows the game to respond to a player's actions.

A game's code includes instructions that control what players can see and do.

None of this would be possible without video game coders. These people write code, or instructions for a computer, to create the game. They choose what controls players will use. They plan the game's levels and ending. In fact, code makes every part of a video game work.

GAME DESIGN

Some video games are developed by just one person. More often, though, a game is a team effort. The team includes programmers, or people who write code. But it also includes game designers, artists, and more. All these people work together to create the game.

Before writing code for a video game, people plan the game's setting, characters, and goals.

Every video game starts with an idea. Often, the idea is a story. The story may be based on a book or movie. Or the game may have a story that is all its own.

Once the team chooses an idea, people begin designing the parts of the game. This stage of the game development process is known as pre-production. Designers create a **storyboard**. They choose what the characters will look like. They also plan the game's goals.

During this stage, the team designs each level of the game. The team plans how the level will look, what objects or characters it will include, and how a player will complete it. Later,

Coders plan each level so players can move through it in a way that is interesting and fun.

programmers will write the code that **implements** this design.

The team comes up with the gameplay mechanics as well. Gameplay mechanics control how the game will be played. Designers choose how each character will move. And they choose what buttons or keys a player will use for each action.

They also plan how each character will interact with other objects in the game. For example, a character might be able to stand on a house but not on a cloud.

Next, coders create a prototype. A prototype is an early, incomplete version of the game. It gives coders a sense of what the game will be like. They use the prototype to test their ideas. It helps them see what works and what doesn't. For example, coders might test a level as they design it. They make sure each object appears where it is supposed to.

Coders fix any problems they find. They make sure the controls work well. Sometimes, they even change the game's design based on what they learn while testing. They work to make the game fun to play.

SAMPLE GAMEPLAY MECHANICS

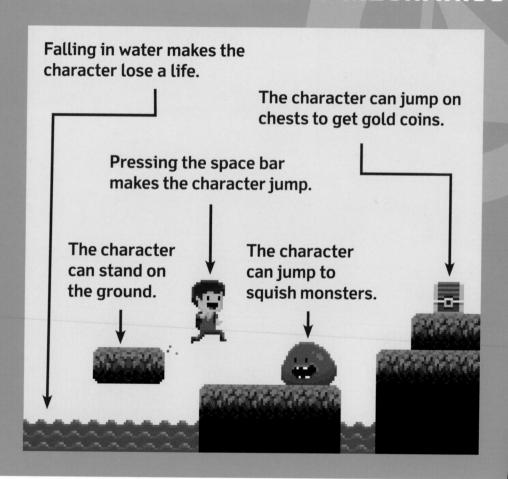

Falling in water makes the character lose a life.

The character can jump on chests to get gold coins.

Pressing the space bar makes the character jump.

The character can stand on the ground.

The character can jump to squish monsters.

CHAPTER 3

BRINGING THE GAME TO LIFE

Next comes the production stage. This stage is when the team creates code to control all the images and sounds in the game. Coders use **programming languages** to do this. There are many different programming languages. Coders choose one to fit the type of game they're making and the device players will use.

Coders use programming languages to create instructions for computers.

In a sports game, the game engine controls what happens when a character kicks a ball.

Languages such as C++ and Java are popular for video games.

Many coders use game engines. A game engine is a **software** tool that helps people create a game. It controls how the game's objects and characters move and interact. Coders give each object **traits** and **properties**. Then they add the object to the game engine. The game engine uses these details to run the game's code.

For instance, in a soccer game, the ball is one object. Its properties tell the game engine what should happen when the ball hits something. The game engine makes the ball stop, roll, or bounce. It also controls how fast and far the ball moves.

HIDING EASTER EGGS

Easter eggs are surprises buried in a game's code. They appear when a player completes a certain set of actions. Some Easter eggs are jokes. Some are references to movies or pop culture. Others are treasures players can collect. Coders have been hiding Easter eggs in video games since the 1970s.

RENDERING

Rendering is the process of turning the game's **elements** into images on the screen. The result often looks similar to an animated movie. Usually, rendering is done by the game engine. It often shows the objects from the player's point of view.

First, the game's creators write code for each object that will appear in the game. Then they add the object to the game engine. The game engine uses these objects to create a map of the whole game. Coders can click and drag to add an object to a particular location on the map.

Then the game engine creates the images the player will see. It adjusts the images to give the scene depth. Objects close to the player are larger and darker. Objects farther away are smaller and lighter. The game engine changes the objects as the player moves through the game. In addition, coders can change the angle that objects are

Rendering often adds shadows to make objects and settings in video games look real.

viewed from. This is similar to changing the camera angle when filming a movie. Coders can also change the scene's lighting. The game engine adjusts the images to respond to these changes.

CHAPTER 4

TYPES OF CODERS

For some video games, one person does several kinds of coding. Coders on larger teams tend to be more specialized. Each coder works on just one part of the game. Physics coders, for example, focus on gameplay mechanics. They make rules about movement in the game. They may write code that **simulates** gravity.

Physics coders help control how objects in a game will move.

Or they may work on what happens when two objects hit each other. Do the objects crash and stop moving? Or do they bounce? If the objects bounce, where do they go?

Artificial intelligence (AI) coders help create code that controls the characters players interact with. Players may talk to or fight with these characters. AI coders shape how the characters respond. They try to make the characters seem real.

User interface coders focus on how players interact with the game. They create the menus that players will see. They choose what options each menu includes. And they code what happens

Menus often appear at the start or end of a level.

when players select each option. Coders try to make the game easy for players to use and understand.

Audio coders add music and sound effects to the game. They make sure the right audio plays at the right time. For example, an arrow might make a sound each time it hits a target. Or creepy music might play when an enemy appears onscreen.

TOOLS PROGRAMMERS

Some coders do not work on the video game itself. Instead, they create tools for other game developers to use. These tools help developers do their jobs more quickly and easily. For example, tools can help artists import their work into the game. Tools can also make it easier to create new levels.

Hundreds of people around the world can play the same online video game at one time.

Network coders write code that connects a video game to the internet. That way, friends can play together even when they're not in the same place. Network coders also think about security. They make sure players cannot see other players' private information. They also try to prevent players from cheating.

CHAPTER 5

FINISHING TOUCHES

When the coding is done, the game enters the post-production phase. The completed code forms an alpha version of the game. This is the first fully working version of the game. The alpha version is given to the test department. Testers play the game. They look for bugs, or flaws in the program.

Some companies send early versions of games to video game conventions for people to test.

Some bugs may cause the game to crash or stop working. Others may just be annoying to players. Coders fix the most important bugs first.

After fixing the main problems, coders release a beta version of the game. This version goes back to the test department. It may also be sent to outside testers. These are regular players who help test the game.

Beta testers note any bugs they find. They also tell developers what they like and dislike about the game. Developers decide which problems to fix before they release the final version. Then the game is ready for the public to buy and play.

STAGES OF VIDEO GAME DEVELOPMENT

1. Pre-production

- Create the story and characters
- Decide the game's goals and gameplay mechanics
- Design each level to make an overall blueprint
- Create and test a prototype

2. Production

- Create art and animations for characters, settings, and objects
- Write and record audio (script, soundtrack, sound effects, etc.)
- Code the game
- Begin testing parts of the game

3. Post-production

- Create and test alpha and beta versions
- Identify and correct bugs
- Complete a final version of the game
- Manufacture and distribute the completed game

FOCUS ON
VIDEO GAME CODING

Write your answers on a separate piece of paper.

1. Write a sentence summarizing the main ideas in Chapter 3.

2. Which stage of video game development would you most want to work on? Why?

3. During which stage is a beta version of the game released?

    A. pre-production
    B. production
    C. post-production

4. Which type of coder would help create the buttons players can click to save or restart the game?

    A. network coder
    B. physics coder
    C. user interface coder

Answer key on page 32.

GLOSSARY

consoles
Computer systems made specifically for video games.

elements
The basic parts of something, such as the objects and characters that make up a video game.

implements
Carries out or brings to completion.

programming languages
Ways of writing instructions so that a computer can understand them.

properties
Details telling how a character or object should react to events.

simulates
Creates an imitation of something.

software
Computer programs that perform certain functions.

storyboard
A series of drawings used to plan out the important events in a story.

traits
Details telling how a character or object should look.

TO LEARN MORE

BOOKS

Bedell, Jane M. *So, You Want to Be a Coder?* New York: Aladdin, 2016.

Slingerland, Janet. *Coding Creations*. Vero Beach, FL: Rourke Educational Media, 2018.

Smibert, Angie. *All About Coding*. Lake Elmo, MN: Focus Readers, 2017.

NOTE TO EDUCATORS

Visit **www.focusreaders.com** to find lesson plans, activities, links, and other resources related to this title.

INDEX

alpha version, 27, 29
artificial intelligence coders, 22
audio coders, 24

beta version, 28–29
bugs, 27–29

characters, 10–13, 16, 22, 29

game engine, 16–17, 18–19

gameplay mechanics, 11, 13, 21, 29

levels, 7, 10, 12, 24, 29

network coders, 25

objects, 10, 12, 16–17, 18, 22, 29

physics coders, 21–22
post-production, 27–29

pre-production, 10–13, 29
production, 15–17, 29
programming languages, 15–16
prototype, 12, 29

rendering, 18

testing, 12–13, 27–29

user interface coders, 22–23